THIRD-PARTY RISK MANAGEMENT

TABLE OF CONTENTS

CHAPTER 1

INTRODUCTION TO THIRD-PARTY RISK MANAGEMENT

Third-party risk management is the process of identifying, assessing, and mitigating risks associated with relationships and interactions with external entities such as suppliers, service providers, contractors, and other business partners. The goal of third-party risk management is to ensure that organizations are protected from potential harm or loss resulting from these relationships. Third-party risk management is a critical component of overall risk management and governance for organizations. It helps organizations understand the potential risks associated with third-party relationships and take proactive measures to mitigate those risks.

Third-party risk management involves a variety of activities, including due diligence and onboarding, contract management, risk assessment, incident response and management, data privacy and security, and cybersecurity. Effective third-party risk management requires collaboration and communication across multiple departments, including legal, procurement, risk management, information technology, and more. The importance of third-party risk management is increasingly recognized in today's business environment, where organizations are relying more and more on third parties to support their operations and achieve their goals. By incorporating best practices in third-party risk management, organizations can mitigate risk and protect their reputation, financial stability, and customer trust.

CHAPTER 2

IDENTIFYING AND ASSESSING THIRD-PARTY RISKS

The first step in effective third-party risk management is identifying and assessing the risks associated with third-party relationships. This requires a thorough understanding of the third party's operations, processes, systems, and data protection measures.

Techniques for identifying third-party risks include conducting a risk assessment, reviewing financial reports and other publicly available information, and conducting site visits or on-site assessments. Third-party risk assessments should be performed on a regular basis and should be updated whenever there is a change in the relationship or when new information becomes available.

When assessing third-party risk, organizations should consider a variety of criteria, including the third party's financial stability, operational stability, and regulatory compliance. Other factors to consider include the third party's security measures, privacy policies, and overall business practices.

Organizations should also evaluate the impact of a potential breach or loss associated with the third party and assess the likelihood of such an event occurring. This requires a deep understanding of the third party's systems and processes, as well as the data and systems that the third party has access to.

Overall, the goal of identifying and assessing third-party risks is to ensure that organizations have a complete and accurate understanding of the risks associated with their third-party relationships. This knowledge is critical for developing effective risk mitigation strategies and for making informed decisions about third-party relationships.

CHAPTER 3

DUE DILIGENCE AND ONBOARDING PROCESS

Due diligence is a critical component of third-party risk management, as it helps organizations understand the risks associated with a potential third-party relationship before entering into an agreement. The due diligence process involves a thorough investigation of the third party's operations, systems, and processes to determine whether it is an appropriate fit for the organization.

The due diligence process should include a review of financial reports, legal and regulatory compliance, security measures, and privacy policies. Additionally, organizations should consider the third party's reputation and track record, as well as any history of breaches or incidents.

Once the due diligence process is complete and a third party has been selected, the onboarding process begins. The onboarding process should include the development of a detailed contract, which outlines the terms and conditions of the relationship, as well as the expectations and obligations of each party.

The contract should include provisions for security and privacy, incident response, and termination. It should also specify the scope of work and the roles and responsibilities of each party.

The onboarding process should also include the implementation of security and privacy controls, such as access controls, data protection measures, and incident response plans. Additionally, organizations should establish a process for monitoring and reporting on the third-party relationship, and for conducting regular risk assessments.

Overall, the due diligence and onboarding process is a critical component of effective third-party risk management, as it helps organizations establish the foundation for a secure and compliant third-party relationship.

CHAPTER 4

CONTRACT MANAGEMENT AND MONITORING

Once a third-party relationship has been established, contract management and monitoring are critical components of effective third-party risk management. Contract management involves the ongoing administration and enforcement of the contract terms and conditions, as well as the management of any changes to the contract.

Organizations should establish a process for regularly reviewing and updating the contract, as well as for communicating any changes to the third party. This helps to ensure that the contract remains relevant and up-to-date, and that the third-party relationship remains secure and compliant.

In addition to contract management, organizations should also establish a process for monitoring the third-party relationship on an ongoing basis. This includes regularly reviewing the third party's performance, conducting risk assessments, and monitoring for potential incidents or breaches.

Organizations should also establish a process for reporting and communicating any incidents or breaches to the appropriate parties, including legal, risk management, and information security teams. This helps to ensure that incidents are quickly identified and properly addressed, and that the organization is able to respond effectively in the event of a breach.

Overall, contract management and monitoring are critical components of effective third-party risk management, as they help organizations maintain control and oversight over their third-party relationships. By implementing best practices in contract management and monitoring, organizations can ensure that their third-party relationships are secure, compliant, and aligned with their overall risk management goals.

CONTRACT MANAGEMENT BEST PRACTICES:

- **Regular Review and Update:** Organizations should establish a process for regularly reviewing and updating the contract, as well as for communicating any changes to the third party. This helps to ensure that the contract remains relevant and up-to-date, and that the third-party relationship remains secure and compliant.

- **Clear Terms and Conditions:** The contract should include clear terms and conditions that outline the expectations and obligations of each party. This helps to ensure that both parties understand their responsibilities and are able to fulfill their obligations effectively.

- **Provisions for Security and Privacy:** The contract should include provisions for security and privacy, such as access controls, data protection measures, and incident response plans. This helps to ensure that sensitive information is protected and that the organization is able to respond effectively in the event of a breach.

- **Roles and Responsibilities:** The contract should specify the roles and responsibilities of each party, including the scope of work and the expectations for performance. This helps to ensure that each party is aware of their obligations and is able to fulfill their responsibilities effectively.

- **Termination Clause:** The contract should include a termination clause that outlines the conditions under which the contract can be terminated, as well as the process for terminating the relationship. This helps to ensure that the organization is able to end the relationship in an orderly and compliant manner if necessary.

- **Monitoring and Reporting:** Organizations should establish a process for monitoring and reporting on the third-party relationship, and for conducting regular risk assessments. This helps to ensure that incidents are quickly identified and properly addressed, and that the organization is able to respond effectively in the event of a breach.

- **Document Management:** Organizations should establish a process for managing and storing contract documents, as well as for ensuring that all parties have access to the latest versions of the contract. This helps to ensure that the contract remains relevant and up-to-date, and that the third-party relationship remains secure and compliant.

CHAPTER 5

THIRD-PARTY RISK ASSESSMENT METHODOLOGIES

Third-party risk assessments are a critical component of effective third-party risk management. These assessments help organizations to identify and evaluate the potential risks associated with a third-party relationship, and to determine the best course of action for managing those risks.

There are several different risk assessment methodologies that organizations can use, including qualitative, quantitative, and hybrid approaches. Each methodology has its own strengths and weaknesses, and organizations should choose the approach that is most appropriate for their specific needs and goals.

SOME COMMON THIRD-PARTY RISK ASSESSMENT METHODOLOGIES INCLUDE:

Qualitative Risk Assessment: Qualitative risk assessments involve the subjective evaluation of potential risks, typically through expert judgment, interviews, or questionnaires. These assessments provide a broad understanding of the risks associated with a third-party relationship, and are often used to identify areas for further investigation.

Quantitative Risk Assessment: Quantitative risk assessments involve the numerical evaluation of potential risks, typically through statistical analysis or simulation. These assessments provide a more precise understanding of the risks associated with a third-party relationship and are often used to determine the financial impact of those risks.

Hybrid Risk Assessment: Hybrid risk assessments combine qualitative and quantitative approaches, providing a comprehensive understanding of the risks associated with a third-party relationship. These assessments often involve a combination of expert judgment, interviews, questionnaires, and statistical analysis.

Regardless of the methodology used, third-party risk assessments should be conducted regularly to ensure that the organization remains aware of the potential risks associated with its third-party relationships, and to enable effective risk management.

Organizations should also consider the use of risk assessment tools, such as automated risk assessment software or cloud-based platforms, to simplify the risk assessment process and ensure consistent and accurate results. By implementing best practices in third-party risk assessment, organizations can effectively manage their third-party risks and ensure the success of their third-party relationships.

CHAPTER 6

THIRD-PARTY INCIDENT RESPONSE AND MANAGEMENT

Incidents involving third-party partners can have a significant impact on an organization, so it's crucial to have a well-defined incident response plan in place. This plan should outline the steps that the organization will take in the event of a breach, data loss, or other incident, and should ensure that the organization is able to respond quickly and effectively.

BEST PRACTICES FOR THIRD-PARTY INCIDENT RESPONSE AND MANAGEMENT INCLUDE:

Pre-planning: Organizations should develop and test a comprehensive incident response plan well before an incident occurs. This plan should include clear roles and responsibilities, as well as procedures for communication, investigation, and resolution.

Rapid Response: Organizations should respond quickly and efficiently to incidents involving third parties, and should prioritize the protection of sensitive data and systems. This may involve isolating affected systems, revoking access, or conducting a forensic investigation.

Collaboration with Third Parties: Organizations should work closely with third-party partners to respond to incidents, and should communicate regularly to ensure that all parties are aware of the situation and working together effectively.

Root Cause Analysis: Organizations should conduct a thorough root cause analysis to determine the cause of the incident and identify any areas for improvement in the third-party relationship or the incident response plan.

Reporting and Documentation: Organizations should document all incidents involving third parties, including the response and resolution, and should report any breaches or data losses to the relevant authorities.

Continuous Improvement: Organizations should use lessons learned from incidents to continuously improve their third-party incident response and management processes, and should regularly review and update their incident response plans to ensure that they remain effective.

By implementing best practices for third-party incident response and management, organizations can minimize the impact of incidents and ensure that their third-party relationships remain secure and compliant.

CHAPTER 7

DATA PRIVACY AND SECURITY

Data privacy and security are crucial considerations in any third-party relationship, as organizations must protect sensitive information and ensure that it is handled in accordance with relevant laws and regulations.

BEST PRACTICES FOR DATA PRIVACY AND SECURITY IN THIRD-PARTY RELATIONSHIPS INCLUDE:

Data Classification: Organizations should classify data based on its level of sensitivity, and should ensure that only authorized personnel have access to sensitive information.

Data Sharing Agreements: Organizations should enter into data sharing agreements with third parties that outline the terms and conditions for the handling of sensitive information.

Encryption: Organizations should encrypt sensitive data, both in transit and at rest, to ensure that it is protected from unauthorized access or interception.

Access Controls: Organizations should implement access controls to ensure that only authorized personnel have access to sensitive information.

Vulnerability Management: Organizations should regularly assess the security of their systems and networks, and should implement measures to address any vulnerabilities that are identified.

Regular Monitoring: Organizations should monitor third-party relationships regularly to ensure that data privacy and security standards are being met.

Incident Response: Organizations should have a well-defined incident response plan in place to respond to security incidents involving third parties, and should take appropriate action to protect sensitive information.

By implementing best practices for data privacy and security, organizations can ensure that their third-party relationships are secure and that sensitive information is handled appropriately.

CHAPTER 8

CYBERSECURITY AND IT RISKS

Cybersecurity and IT risks are major concerns in any third-party relationship, as organizations must protect their systems and data from cyber-attacks and other security threats.

BEST PRACTICES FOR MANAGING CYBERSECURITY AND IT RISKS IN THIRD-PARTY RELATIONSHIPS INCLUDE:

Cybersecurity Due Diligence: Organizations should conduct thorough cybersecurity due diligence on potential third-party partners, including a review of their security posture, systems, and policies.

IT Risk Assessments: Organizations should conduct regular IT risk assessments of their third-party relationships to identify and mitigate potential security threats.

Contractual Requirements: Organizations should include cybersecurity and IT requirements in their contracts with third parties, and should monitor compliance with these requirements.

Incident Response Planning: Organizations should have a well-defined incident response plan in place to respond to cyber-attacks and other security incidents involving third parties.

Cybersecurity Awareness Training: Organizations should provide cybersecurity awareness training to their employees and third-party partners to help prevent security incidents.

Regular Vulnerability Scanning: Organizations should regularly scan their systems and networks **for vulnerabilities, and should implement measures to address any issues that are identified.**

Network Segmentation: Organizations should implement network segmentation to reduce the risk of cyber-attacks and to protect sensitive data and systems.

By implementing best practices for managing cybersecurity and IT risks in third-party relationships, organizations can reduce their exposure to security threats and ensure the protection of their systems and data.

CHAPTER 9

COMMON INTERVIEW QUESTIONS AND ANSWERS FOR THIRD-PARTY RISK ANALYSTS

Interviewer: How do you approach third-party due diligence and onboarding?

Response : I take a thorough and methodical approach to third-party due diligence and onboarding. This includes a review of the third party's business practices, financial stability, and security posture, as well as a review of their contracts and policies. I also work closely with other departments, such as legal and IT, to ensure that all risks are properly assessed and mitigated.

Interviewer: Can you walk us through your approach to incident response and management in a third-party relationship?

Response : My approach to incident response and management involves a clear and well-defined process, including incident identification, triage, and investigation. I work closely with other departments, such as legal and IT, to ensure that the incident is thoroughly investigated and that appropriate action is taken to mitigate the risk. I also regularly review and update our incident response plan to ensure that it is effective and up-to-date.

Interviewer: How do you ensure that third-party relationships are in compliance with relevant laws and regulations?

Response : I regularly review and assess our third-party relationships to ensure that they are in compliance with relevant laws and regulations, such as data privacy and security regulations. I also work closely with legal and other departments to ensure that our contracts and policies are up-to-date and in compliance with relevant laws and regulations.

Interviewer: How do you prioritize and manage your workload when dealing with multiple third-party relationships?

Response : I prioritize my workload by first assessing the level of risk associated with each third-party relationship and then determining which ones require the most immediate attention. I also use project management tools and techniques to ensure that I am able to effectively manage my workload and meet all deadlines.

Interviewer: Can you describe your experience with contract negotiation and management with third parties?

Response : I have extensive experience with contract negotiation and management, and have successfully negotiated favorable terms with a variety of third-party vendors. I also regularly review and assess our contracts to ensure that they are up-to-date and in compliance with our policies and procedures.

Interviewer: How do you communicate and collaborate with other departments and stakeholders in managing third-party risks?

Response : I have excellent communication and collaboration skills, and regularly work with other departments, such as legal and IT, to

Interviewer: Can you explain your experience with identifying and assessing third-party risk?

Response: I have worked in the field of third-party risk management for several years, during which time I have developed a thorough understanding of the various risks that organizations may face when working with third parties. I am experienced in using risk assessment frameworks and tools to identify and evaluate potential risks, and in developing and implementing risk management plans to mitigate those risks.

Interviewer: How do you stay current with the latest developments in third-party risk management?

Response: I stay current with the latest developments in third-party risk management through a combination of continuing education, industry research, and networking with other professionals in the field. I also attend relevant conferences and workshops to stay informed of new best practices and regulatory changes.

Interviewer: Can you give an example of a time when you had to manage a particularly challenging third-party risk?

Response: I once worked with a company that was outsourcing a critical business process to a third party. During the due diligence process, we identified several potential risks, including data security and regulatory compliance concerns. I worked closely with the third party to address these risks and implement appropriate controls, and we were able to successfully implement the outsourcing arrangement without any major issues.

Interviewer: How do you ensure that third-party risks are effectively communicated to senior management?

Response: Effective communication is key to managing third-party risks. I ensure that risks are effectively communicated to senior management by using clear and concise language and providing them with relevant information such as risk assessments, mitigation plans, and key performance indicators. I also schedule regular meetings to update senior management on the status of third-party risks and any issues that may arise.

Interviewer: What is your approach to vendor management?

Response: My approach to vendor management is to establish clear expectations and guidelines for third parties, and to regularly monitor their performance to ensure that they are meeting those expectations. I also conduct regular risk assessments to identify potential risks and take appropriate action to mitigate them.

Interviewer: How do you handle a situation where a third party is not meeting its contractual obligations?

Response: In the event that a third party is not meeting its contractual obligations, I would first assess the impact of the non-compliance on the organization and then communicate the issue to the third party. I would then work with the third party to develop a plan to address the issue and bring them back into compliance. If the issue cannot be resolved, I would work with legal and senior management to consider termination of the contract.

Interviewer: What are your thoughts on the importance of data privacy in third-party risk management?

Response: Data privacy is a critical component of third-party risk management. I believe that organizations have a responsibility to protect personal data and to ensure that third parties handling this data are doing so in a secure and compliant manner. I make sure to include data privacy considerations in all my risk assessments and vendor management activities.

Interviewer: How do you ensure that third-party risks are integrated into an organization's overall risk management strategy?

Response: To ensure that third-party risks are integrated into an organization's overall risk management strategy, I work closely with other risk management functions, such as information security and compliance, to understand their risks and objectives. I also make sure to align third-party risk management activities with the organization's overall risk appetite and risk management framework.

Interviewer: Can you explain your experience with regulatory compliance in the context of third-party risk management?

Response: I have experience working with a variety of regulations that are relevant to third-party such as GDPR for European data, and CCPA for privacy act in California USA

Interviewer: Can you explain your experience with conducting third-party risk assessments?

Response: I have experience conducting risk assessments for potential vendors and partners, including reviewing their security policies and controls, evaluating their financial stability, and assessing their overall risk to our organization.

Interviewer: How do you stay up to date on industry regulations and standards related to third-party risk management?

Response: I stay current by regularly reading industry publications, attending relevant conferences and events, and participating in professional associations or online communities focused on third-party risk management.

Interviewer: Can you describe a time when you had to handle a high-risk third-party situation?

Response: In my previous role, a vendor we were working with experienced a data breach. I led the response team, which included assessing the extent of the breach, communicating with relevant stakeholders, and implementing additional security controls to prevent future breaches.

Interviewer: How do you prioritize and manage multiple third-party risks at the same time?

Response: I prioritize risks based on their likelihood and potential impact to the organization. I then create a plan to address the highest-priority risks first and continually re-evaluate the risks and adjust the plan as needed.

Interviewer: How do you ensure that third-party vendors are meeting their compliance obligations?

Response: I regularly review vendor compliance documentation, conduct on-site assessments and audits, and implement ongoing monitoring processes to ensure vendors are meeting their compliance obligations.

Interviewer: How do you evaluate the effectiveness of controls put in place to mitigate third-party risks?

Response: I conduct periodic assessments and testing to evaluate the effectiveness of controls. I also track and analyze metrics, such as incident response time and remediation efforts, to identify areas for improvement.

Interviewer: Can you discuss your experience with creating and implementing third-party risk management policies?

Response: I have experience in creating and implementing policies and procedures for third-party risk management, including vendor due diligence, incident response, and ongoing monitoring.

Interviewer: How do you communicate third-party risk information to senior management and the board of directors?

Response: I present risk information in a clear and concise manner, highlighting key risks, the impact to the organization, and any recommended actions. I also provide regular updates on the status of risk management efforts.

Interviewer: How do you handle conflicts with third parties regarding risk management?

Response: I approach conflicts with a mindset of finding a mutually beneficial solution. I communicate clearly and objectively, outlining the risks and any potential impact to the organization. I also consider the vendor's perspective and work to find a compromise that addresses the organization's concerns while also being reasonable for the vendor.

Interviewer: Can you give an example of a successful third-party risk management program you have implemented in the past?

Response: I implemented a third-party risk management program at my previous company that included regular vendor assessments, incident response plans, and ongoing monitoring processes. The program helped the company identify and mitigate potential risks and improve overall vendor security posture.

Interviewer: Can you give an example of a time you disagree with business on vendor risk assessment score

Response: I previously reviewed a vendor questionnaire and discovered they claimed to have passed a SOC 2 report. Upon further investigation, I found they needed a current SOC 2 report. I brought this to the attention of the business and asked that they acknowledge the risk in writing. This prompted the company to follow up with the vendor, and we discovered they still needed an updated SOC 2 report. I requested that the vendor provide an updated report before we continued doing business with them. Ultimately, the company appreciated my efforts to prevent us from being exposed to unnecessary risk

CONCLUSION

In conclusion, effective third-party risk management is critical in today's business landscape. This book has covered various aspects of the field, from identifying and assessing risks to incident response and management, and from contract management to data privacy and cybersecurity. The best practices and insights shared in this book can help organizations ensure the safety and security of their data, as well as the success of their third-party relationships.

As technology continues to advance, the importance of third-party risk management will only increase. Emerging technologies such as artificial intelligence and machine learning are poised to have a significant impact on the field, and it is essential for professionals to stay informed and adapt to these changes.

In the future, organizations must remain vigilant in their risk management practices, continuously updating their methodologies and tools to stay ahead of new threats. This requires ongoing professional development, collaboration, and a commitment to continuous improvement.

We hope that this book has been a valuable resource for anyone interested in the field of third-party risk management. We encourage you to continue learning and growing in this field, and to seek out the guidance and support of experienced professionals. Thank you for your time and attention.

Made in the USA
Middletown, DE
19 December 2024

67756646R00015